The ART OF TOUCH

A Massage Manual for Young People

The ART OF TOUCH

A Massage Manual for Young People

Chia Martin

Photographs by Sheila Mitchell

HOHM PRESS
Prescott, Arizona

Printed in the United States of America.

Library of Congress # 95-077754
ISBN # 0-934252-57-2

Hohm Press, P.O. Box 2501
Prescott, AZ 86302
(520) 778-9189

The theories and instructions in this book are expressed as the author's opinion
and are not meant to be used to diagnose, prescribe or administer
in any manner to any physical ailments. In any matters related to your health,
please contact a qualified, licensed health practitioner.

Design and Typesetting: Shukyo Lin Rainey

for
Gita, Anna and Meghan

Acknowledgements

I would like to thank my editors, Regina and Rose, for their attention to details.
Thanks to Becky and Shukyo for their tireless patience.
Thanks to Rita and Michelle for their help in arranging all the photo sessions,
and to Sarah Perletz, Kira Wolfson, and Prisceillia Mancha, superb models.

And my deepest gratitude to my teacher, Lee. All I offer comes from Him.

CONTENTS

PREFACE

One cold and rainy afternoon I heard a knock at my door. "Come quick to the schoolroom . . .And bring a quarter!" Joe, the ten-year-old who beckoned me, was so bright, so excited, that within moments I had my two-year-old on my hip and my quarter in hand. When I arrived at our neighborhood homeschool, the sign on the door read: "Massage: Come On In." We entered to the sounds of soft music and muffled giggles. Anna, Gita, Jacob and the rest of the children had created a space that was truly inviting. They had dimmed the lights and made small rooms with sheets as dividers. It was womb-like, comfortable. Incense filled the air, candlelight flickered. Jacob asked if I would like a neck massage, foot massage or full-body massage. (Of course, my two-year-old was enchanted.) After paying my quarter I was led to a corner filled with pillows and blankets. Then (in the midst of my daughter's tumbling games among the pillows), I was given one of the sweetest massages I have ever received. I felt nurtured from the top of my head, to the tips of my toes, to the depths of my soul.

Massage is an experience of relationship. Whether it is two friends, parent and child, or whether we are simply nurturing ourselves, massage has the power to open places that are closed, to stimulate places that are numb, to comfort places that are sore, and to heal places that are hurt. Massage is for all ages. Massage is about caring.

This manual is written for you. Read it, learn from it, share it with your friends, enjoy it, and most of all—have fun!

PART I

Why Massage?

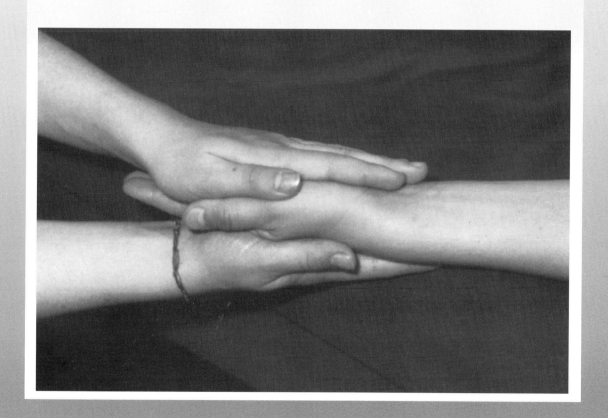

What Is Massage?

Massage is a way of speaking without words, much the same way a smile or hug is. It is also a way of moving energy through the body. Massage is a healing art. Through the act of touching in a special way, massage has the power not only to heal sore and aching muscles, but to calm hurt feelings, and to help unlock stuck energy.

Massage has many different purposes. You may find as you begin to experiment with massage that you experience some or all of these benefits over time, both in giving and receiving massage.

Why Massage?
Ten Good Reasons

1. It feels good.
2. It's fun.
3. It's a great way to give and receive.
4. It helps with aches, pains, stiffness and blood circulation.
5. It is a simple way to learn to communicate without words.
6. It helps us learn to nurture ourselves.
7. It helps prevent illness.
8. It helps build trust, friendship and respect.
9. It helps us learn more about energy currents in the body.
10. It's meditative—creating harmony, balance and inner calmness.

Who <u>Not</u> to Massage

♥ There are times when massage can actually harm more than help.
Here are a few guidelines to follow:

Do not massage anyone who has
1. A fever.
2. A rash.
3. A serious or a contagious illness
such as mumps, measles or mononucleosis.

♥ If you have a question, check with an adult or parent.
Do not try to take the place of a doctor or healer.

———————

PART II

Preparing for Massage

Preparing the Place

1. Find a place that is quiet—inside or outside.

2. Warmth is important. If inside, avoid a space that is drafty or chilly.
If outside, avoid strong full sun for any length of time;
and remember, if in the sun, to cover your head and
particularly the head of the person you are massaging.
Be careful when receiving massage not to fall asleep in direct sunlight.

3. Use a mat or blanket on the floor, or use a massage table,
if you are lucky enough to have one or borrow one.
Beds are usually too soft for an effective massage.
Pads on the floor are better.

4. Make sure you have enough room to move
all the way around the person you are massaging.

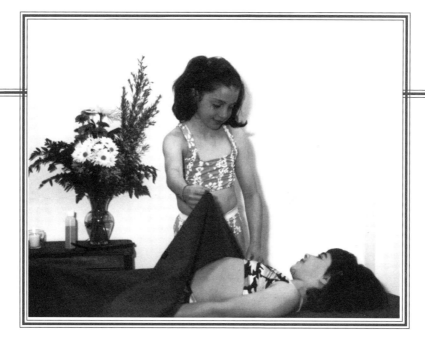

5. Have blankets and sheets ready. (Choose sheets that are okay to get oil on.)
Cover your friend with a large sheet from the neck down making sure
your friend's feet are warm. During the massage expose only the area
you are working on so your friend stays warm.

6. Light a candle and perhaps some incense
to help create a relaxing mood.

7. If you decide to use music, choose music that is soft and gentle.
Just remember that music can be a distraction from a good massage.

8. Have drinking water available for yourself and the person you are massaging.

Preparing Yourself to Give a Massage

1 Washing hands up to and including elbows is an important step both before and after giving a massage.

2 It is best not to give a massage if you are feeling ill or running a fever.

3 If you have long hair, tie it back.

4 Warm up your hands by briskly rubbing them together before you begin.

5 Relax into your own "center" (see section on centering).

6 Pay attention to your posture when massaging so that you don't come away needing a massage yourself. Always keep elbows and knees slightly bent, back straight and one leg in front of the other to keep balance.

7 Massage is best done when both the giver and the receiver don't have a full stomach.

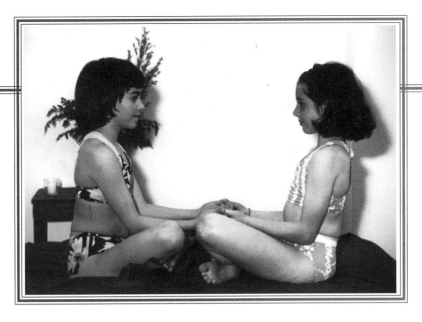

Things to Talk about with Your Friend Before Massage

1. Ask your friend if she or he has any places on the body that are ticklish or painful, places that you should avoid massaging.

2. Check timing with your friend. Know how much time you have. Allow one hour for a full-body massage, then pace yourself. Having to rush at the end of a massage or stop suddenly can upset the quiet and relaxation of the massage.

3. Tell your friend you will honor and respect his or her wishes when it comes to touching. If you do not want to be touched on any part of your body, please say so. The same is true if you do not want to touch any part of someone else's body. Massage is meant to be fun and relaxing. If you cannot trust the person massaging you to honor your wishes, get a massage from someone else. If the person you are massaging insists that you massage him or her in any way that you do not want to, end the massage and do not engage massage with this person anymore. Only do what feels okay to both of you.

4. You may or may not wish to wear clothing while receiving a massage. Suitable clothing for girls might be a swimsuit; for boys, gym shorts. Although massage can be performed through clothing, the effectiveness of the massage is lessened. Talk it over.

Finding Your "Center"

Finding "center" is finding inner balance, inner harmony. Each of us has his or her own unique center. We never lose this center, but we sometimes lose touch with it. Stress, worry, illness, fear, anger and other physical or emotional states can cause us to stumble, to feel confused or out of balance. It is very helpful to be able to find your center again. Paying attention to breathing is a simple way to find center. (We'll talk more about breath later.) You can also use your mind to make visualizations—mental pictures that help you relax. Visualizations are one of the most interesting and imaginative ways to find your center and stay there, for as long as you wish.

Visualization Exercises
For Centering

♥ *Visualizations* ♥
A visualization is a fantasy
or picture in your imagination.
It is a way to use your mind
to help relax your body.
Visualizations can be spoken softly
while you give a massage.
You may also find yourself
using this technique to fall asleep
or calm your mind before a test
or sports competition.
The following visualizations are examples
you can use to help your friend relax
while you give her or him a massage.
They can also help you to relax
into a centered state before beginning
to give the massage.

The Lake

Imagine the mind as a large body of water: water as far as the eye can see.
The water is the bluest of blues and runs deep and pure.
As thoughts begin to rise or tensions are felt,
see them as waves upon this water—some large, some smaller.
As you begin to relax more deeply, using the breath,
imagine these thoughts or waves washing onto the shore,
spreading out like fingers, then disappearing or melting into the sand,
until the lake becomes still with only a few ripples
here and there that gently blend into the water's surface.
All is clear. All is peaceful. All is serene.

♥ ♥ ♥

Clouds

Imagine you are lying on your back on a green grassy hill
in the warm sunshine, gazing at a beautiful blue sky.
Then imagine your mind as this expansive, limitless sky.
Notice the clouds rolling up and drifting by.
As thoughts, tensions or worries arise, see them as these banks
of clouds floating past the mind's eye almost like a movie.
One minute you see their distinct shapes, sizes and depths, the next minute
their shapes have changed and they have moved out of your vision.
Try watching this imaginary sky. Look past the clouds and into the sky
so that eventually you don't even notice the clouds.
Blue as far as the eye can see.
Restful. Healing. Expansive.

♥ ♥ ♥

13

Breath & Massage

Our breath is one of the greatest tools we have,
and one of the easiest to take for granted.

"The life force in the body (prana)
is derived from the air we inhale.
This life energy is the food of the mind.
When sufficient life energy
is produced through proper breathing,
the mind grows stronger and sharper."

—Baba Hari Das, *A Child's Garden of Yoga*

♥ ♥ ♥

How to Use the Breath during Massage

For the massage giver:

♥ Listen to your breath flowing in and out. You may remind your friend, in a gentle voice, to follow the flow of his or her own breath or to use the breath to help let go of tension, especially when you find tense places in his or her body. You can try breathing as often as your friend does, or you can breathe more deeply and slowly as a way to remind your friend to relax. Use intuition (see page 29) in deciding what to do, or ask your friend what he or she prefers.

♥ Use the breath to feel your center—the origin of your own unique inner balance.

♥ Use your breath to help keep an even-paced massage.

For the massage receiver:

♥ Use the breath to help yourself deeply relax each body part your friend touches.

♥ Breathe gently on the inhalation, imagine filling the body with the bright, clean healing energy of *prana*, the life force. Exhale, allow the breath to carry out with it all the worries, aches and pains, tensions and upsets of the day.

♥ As you begin to relax more deeply through massage notice how your breathing changes. Does it become slower, deeper?

♥ Use the breath to feel your center—the origin of your own unique inner balance.

Full Belly Breath

This breathing exercise can be used for relaxation and to renew your energy before a massage (both partners can try it), or before exercise or bed.

♥ Lie on the floor or on a mat, on your back with hands relaxed at your sides, palms down; legs and feet a few inches apart.

♥ Breathe a few regular breaths.

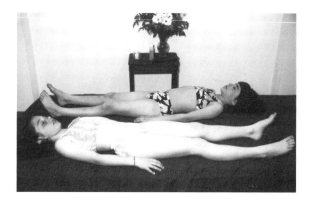

♥ Then, with one long, slow yet steady in-breath imagine that you are filling the belly (abdomen) with air. The belly expands like a balloon.

♥ Slowly release the breath until you feel empty, then push the remaining breath out, hissing like a snake.

♥ Repeat two more times.

PART III

Giving a Massage

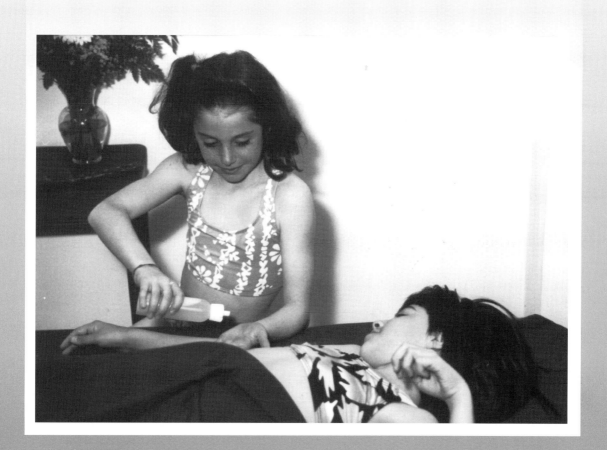

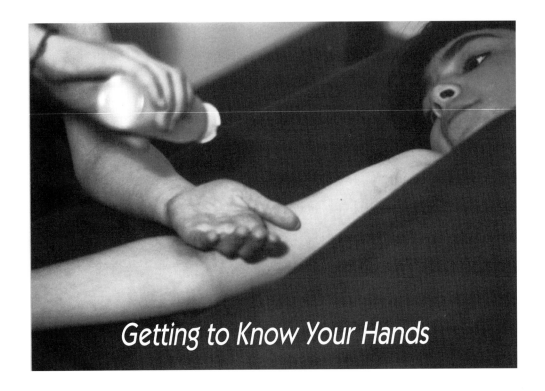

Getting to Know Your Hands

"Knowing how to be at one with your hands is the core of massage, the one real technique. The more massage you do, the more this knowledge will open itself to you. Hands are subtle, however, and getting acquainted with them takes time."
—George Downing, *The Massage Book*

♥ Keep contact with your friend's body once the massage has begun. If you need to break contact to apply oil, keep your elbow or arm in touch with your partner.

♥ Keep your hands relaxed. You may occasionally shake off excess tension that collects or builds up. Shaking the hands helps to loosen them and release any tension you may have collected. (Remember to shake away from your friend.) Massage with the whole hand, not just the fingertips. This will help the hand stay loose.

♥ Apply pressure. Don't be afraid to apply pressure when massaging. Pressure feels good.

Notice the amount of pressure you like when being massaged. If you are afraid you may be hurting your friend, ask. And when receiving massage remember it is important to communicate your needs, likes and dislikes. Always ask your friend to tell you if anything you are doing bothers her or if she wants the pressure heavier or lighter. What is comfortable for your friend is what will provide the most benefit.

♥ Use your entire body. Let your hands be an extension of a full-body movement. Let the energy rise out of your center, through your body and then out your hands.

Blind Massage

An Exercise

Either during a massage or just for fun,
with eyes closed the entire time (5-10 minutes),
let your hands explore your friend:
face, hands, arms, legs, feet, knees and back.
Move your hands lightly across the skin
as a blind person might,
feeling the inside of the ears,
in between the toes,
each vertebrae in the spine.
Ask your hands to be your eyes,
your ears, your heart, your words,
your only tool of communication.

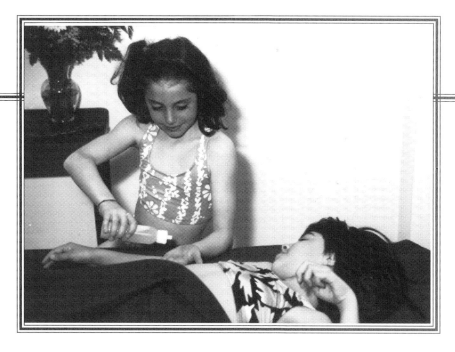

Some Tips about Oil

♥ There are many varieties of massage oil available through bath shops, health food stores and even department stores. Oil needn't be fancy. Simple almond oil or even vegetable oil will work just fine. You may choose to scent it or not—by adding a drop of perfumed oil. Be sure the aroma is pleasing to your friend. Some people prefer lotion.

♥ Put the oil first on your own hands, then place your hands on your friend's body. Do not pour oil directly on your friend's skin.

♥ Use a little oil at a time. Always ask your friend first before applying oil to his or her face.

♥ Apply oil only to the part of the body you are going to work on right away.

♥ Pay attention to where you put the oil bottle down. Keep it close by and remember oil can stain furniture and rugs. A dish or small plate is handy as a base.

♥ Try to keep some part of your body always touching your friend even when applying oil. Use elbows or back of arm to maintain contact.

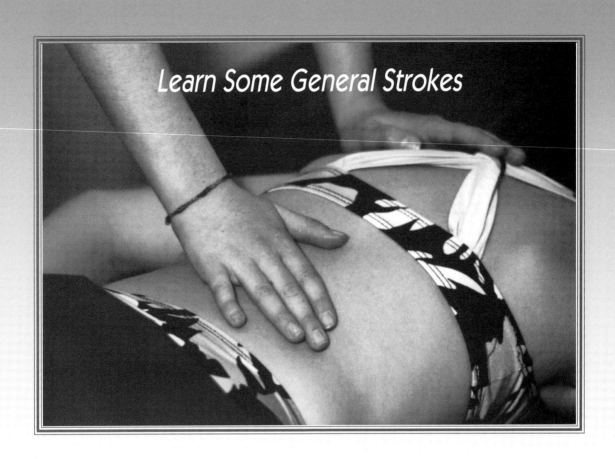

Learn Some General Strokes

There are many types of touch or strokes used in massage. Three basic strokes are suggested here, with directions for how to use them. You can combine them or use them separately in working on most parts of the body. Additional strokes will also be taught throughout the book. Practice the general strokes first so that you feel comfortable in using them. Have fun learning the additional strokes.

♥ **Effleurage** (*ef-lur-aj*)—Light touch. This is a friendly touch that relaxes and helps build trust. This stroke helps prepare the body for deeper massage. This is a stroke to use at the beginning of your massage. To do effleurage use your hands lightly (palm and fingers) to make smooth, gliding motions over the skin. These strokes encourage circulation and feed blood to the skin.

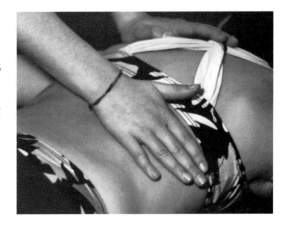

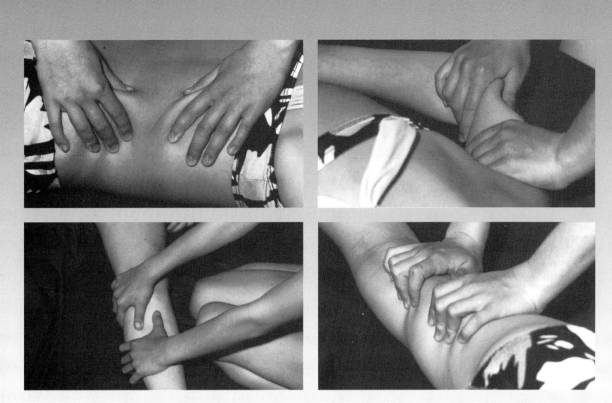

♥ **Petrissage** (*pet-ra-saj*)—Deeper touch. This stroke reaches the muscles and helps to release deep tension. It uses thumbs, fingers and the whole hand to knead the muscles and move them away from the bone. It may include squeezing, rolling, and wringing motions. This also increases circulation, moves tension out of the muscles, and gets food to the cells. Always follow this with effleurage.

♥ **Tapping or cupping**—Tapping may be done to any part of the body. It is best used at the end of massage. Tapping is lightly drumming the fingertips or cupping the whole hand. You may do this by tapping with the whole hand as if you were knocking with your fingertips. Or you may roll the fingertips as you might on your desk when bored. It is a gentle consistent stroke that helps to break up energy knots. It feels great too! (You may want to practice these strokes on yourself before working with a friend.)

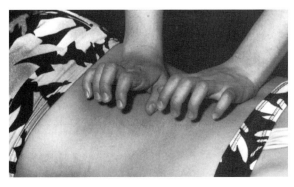

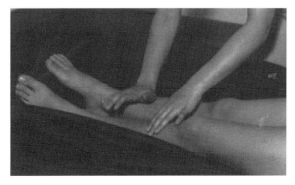

The Massage

Ready to begin? Have your friend lie on her back. Remember to make sure she is warm and comfortably covered with a sheet and blanket. Arms are a good place to start. Uncover the right arm. Tuck the drape or sheet up against her right side.

Arms

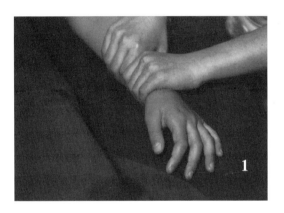

♥ (1) Begin at the wrist. Hold the arm between both hands and gently squeeze the arm all the way up to the shoulder. Do this rather vigorously 5-7 times. (Petrissage.)

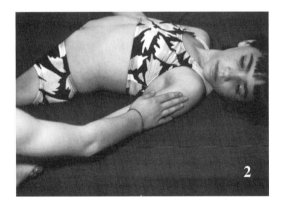

♥ (2) Next use big strokes to do figure 8's all the way up the arm. (Effleurage.)

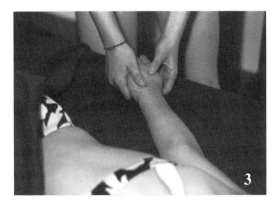

♥ (3) Now, using the same basic stroke as in Step 2, go slower. Use the thumbs to make small circles all the way up. Massage the arm muscles.

Additional Strokes

♥ (1) Use your thumbs to massage around the wrist making small circles.

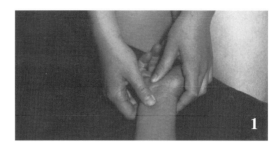

♥ (2) Grip the hand and rotate the wrist slowly. If you feel your friend holding up his/her own hand, encourage her to let it drop— to let you do the work.

♥ (3) Lift the arm and shake it gently, moving it in small circles. Make sure the elbow is bent. You may want to support the elbow with one hand.

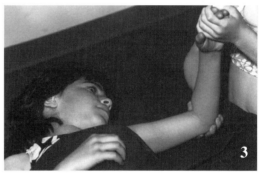

♥ (4) Lay the arm down, raised, so that it lies along the ear. Massage around the arm pit. (Effleurage.)

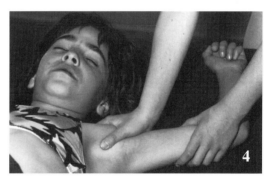

♥ (5) To finish, place one hand on the wrist, the other on the waist, then stretch the arm gently yet firmly away from the body.

Emotional Release

For the massage giver:
Massage can bring release of
emotional tension as well as physical tension.
Sometimes being deeply touched, soothed or nourished
reminds us of places inside that may be lonely, sad or afraid.
It's important to allow for this
if you feel emotions being released.
If you are giving a massage
and your friend begins to release emotional tensions,
to cry, laugh or express uncomfortableness,
ask what you can do.
Allow your friend some time to express
whatever he/she needs to,
and then proceed sensitively.

For the massage receiver:
When you are receiving a massage,
you may experience a release of sad or happy feelings.
You may get a case of the giggles during your massage.
Remember each massage is a new experience.
Don't be afraid to let the feelings arise.
Try to view each new experience as a discovery
of the uniqueness of "you."

Hands

Our hands are one of our most important tools. They are also one of the most sensitive areas of the body. We use our hands to write, to cook, to pray, to catch a football or baseball, to play musical instruments, to express many feelings such as anger, pain, and excitement, to clap and to turn cartwheels. Hands respond most gratefully to lots of TLC (Tender Loving Care). Even though hands do not have lots of muscle, they are fun to massage.

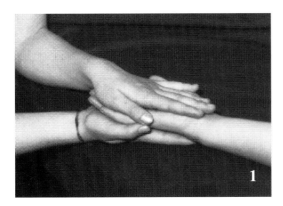

♥ (1) Begin by stroking the whole hand with gentle, even strokes. (Effleurage).

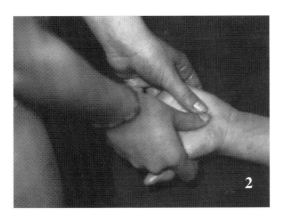

♥ (2) Then use the thumbs to make small circles all over the palm of the hand, the heel and around the wrist. Be sure to massage the knuckles.
♥ Do the same to the back of the hand.

♥ (3) Massage each finger. Stroke the webbing between each finger.

Additional Strokes

♥ (1) Interlock the fingers of your hand with your friend's fingers and stretch the hand. While doing so, use the thumbs of both your hands to massage the palm of your friend's hand.

♥ (2) Find the indentation between the thumb and forefinger. Hold this spot firmly for a count to 10. While holding you may wish to massage the point lightly.

♥ (3) To finish, sandwich your partner's hand between yours. Feel the energy flow between you. Do the same to the other hand.

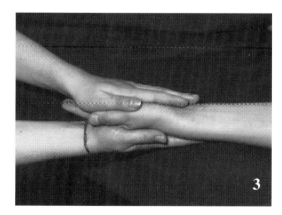

Follow Intuition

Intuition means knowing something
without having to be taught.
It is more like a "gut feeling"
that something is right or necessary.
Remember, following directions exactly
is not what makes a good massage.
A good "massager" is one
who follows his or her intuition,
one who is not afraid to spend extra time
on an area that feels tense or stiff,
one who responds to the body
the way we often wish our mothers,
fathers, and friends would respond
to our waves of feelings
or our problems—by simply listening.
Don't be afraid to follow your intuition
—both when giving and receiving a massage.
This may mean perhaps using more pressure
when you give a massage, or it may mean
stopping earlier than you planned.
Let the body speak, and use massage to help you learn
to listen to the body and to your own intuition.

Legs

Few things feel better than having your legs rubbed. We demand a lot of our legs throughout the day and they love to be thanked with massage. The legs have lots of big muscles so they respond well to deep and big strokes.

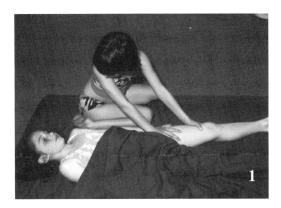

♥ (1) Spread the feet and legs about a foot apart.

♥ You may use similar strokes to those used on the arms. Standing beside the table or sitting near your partner's shoulder, place one hand on the outside of the left thigh just above the knee, the other on the inside. Work the hands up the leg in tandem as though you were pulling a rope over a ledge. Use long, firm strokes. Do this about 10 times. (Effleurage.)

♥ (2) Use the fingertips and thumb to massage the thigh muscles and calf muscles. Knead them as you might knead bread dough.

♥ (3) Starting at your partner's ankle, place your thumbs together, side by side. Lightly grasp the leg just above the ankle, fingers fanning to both sides. (This stroke may remind you of a butterfly.) Then, using firm but gentle pressure "walk" your hands up the leg, massaging as you go, up to the knee and then to the thigh. (Petrissage.)

Additional Strokes

Caution: Knees can be a little tricky. It can feel great to have them massaged. It can also be uncomfortable. Check with your friend about his or her knees either as you go along or before you begin.

♥ (1) The knee: Imagine the knee is a circle. Using thumbs, massage the outside rim of the circle. The thumbs go in opposite directions, starting at the top of the knee and ending at the bottom. Do this 5-6 times.

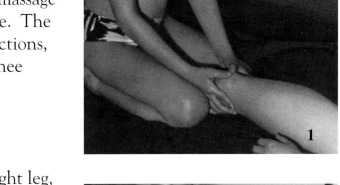

♥ (2) Raise your friend's right leg, placing the right foot parallel to the left knee. Place the palms on either side of the thigh of the right leg with your fingers extending outward. Roll the leg between your hands, as though you were drying your hair or polishing a shoe. Do this back and forth vigorously 5 times. Gently lay the leg down and repeat on the left leg.

♥ (3) After both legs have been massaged, cup your hands under each ankle and pull the legs straight with a firm, even grasp away from the body. This stretches the spine and hips. Count to 10. Release. Then pull 2 more times.

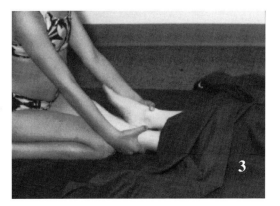

Feet

Our feet are very important. They walk, run, skip, dance, swim, dive, march. They deserve lots of attention and care. If you want to give or receive a massage and only have a few minutes, go for the feet. Tens of thousands of nerve endings are concentrated in the soles of the feet. The opposite ends of these nerves are located throughout the rest of the body. Massaging the feet massages the whole body. See the "Reflexology Chart" on page 57. You will most likely find it fun and interesting. In addition to massage itself, simply going barefoot can stimulate the feet and thereby the whole body.

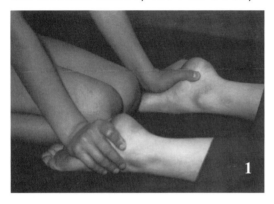

Feet don't need much oil, if any.

♥ (1) Begin by placing one hand on each foot. Make firm contact. Hold for a count of 5. Release.

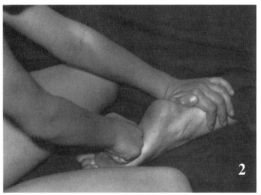

♥ (2) Move to the right foot. Remember to drape the left foot. Make a fist with your right hand. Use the knuckles in a pressing, rolling motion to massage the sole of the foot.

♥ (3) Grasp the foot with both hands. Use the thumbs to make little circles over the whole foot— top and bottom.

♥ 4. Lift the foot. Massage the heel. You may be firm here.

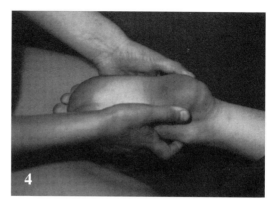

♥ 5. Now massage the toes and between the toes. Remember how you massaged the hand.

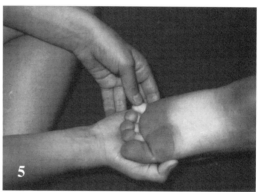

♥ 6. Next hold the foot in the hand with thumbs pointing toward the ankle. Massage the sides of the foot. Move up and down. Finish by stroking down the foot and out the toes.

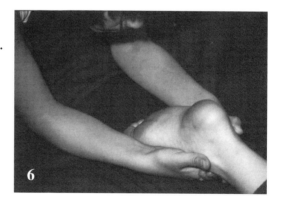

Additional Strokes

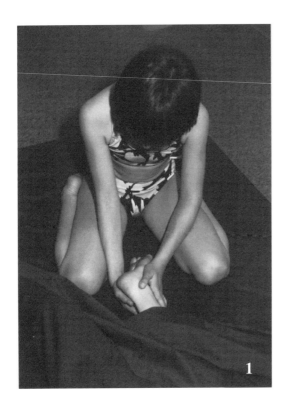

♥ (1) Hold the ankle between the palms of your hands and roll the foot back and forth rather fast, side-to-side.

♥ To finish, hold the foot between your hands. Place one palm on top of the foot, the other underneath. Feel your center.

♥ Go to the left foot and repeat.

Go barefoot more.

Tension Release

When you are receiving a massage, your friend
may work on a place that is sore and aches.
Use your breath to try to relax "into" the pain.
As you breathe deeply into that place,
you may feel tension release and the pain dissolve.
If, on the other hand, the pain is too much,
increases, or causes you to tense up even more,
then ask your friend to move on to another area.
Again, letting your friend know
how you feel is very important.

When giving a massage, watch for frowns, grimaces,
groans or squirming. Remember to ask if you suspect
that something hurts or is uncomfortable.

Back

Now have your friend turn over onto the stomach. If your time is going well and both you and your friend wish to go longer, you may do further massage on the back of the legs and feet before going on to the back itself. Use the same strokes you used on the front of the leg when massaging the back of the leg. *(Caution: Be careful never to put direct pressure on the spine.)*

♥ (1) Glide the hands up the entire back. Rub all over in any direction your hands want to go. End with your hands at the shoulders. (Effleurage.)

When the back feels strong and well, the whole body feels strong and well.

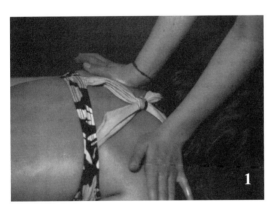

♥ (2) Let your hands "crawl" up the back using the thumbs to massage either side of the spine. Your hands should wrap around the sides so you massage them too.

♥ (3) Move your hands to the lower back. Make big circles moving away from you.

♥ (4) Now go up the spine slowly, using your thumbs to make tiny circles. You can move out from the spine to the rest of the back as well.

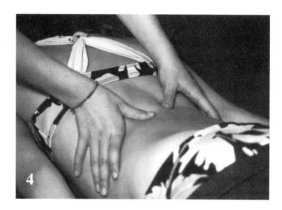

♥ (5) Next massage the shoulders. Do both the top of the shoulders and the shoulder blades. Pinch the muscle that connects the shoulder and neck. Knead it like bread dough. Do both sides at once. (Petrissage)

Additional Strokes

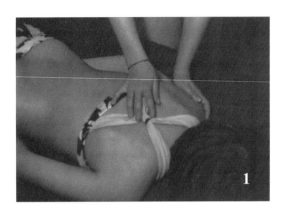

♥ (1) Use the thumb to work all around the shoulder blade. Making circles with the thumb, follow right along the ridge of the blade.

♥ Make big circles on the upper back. (Effleurage.)

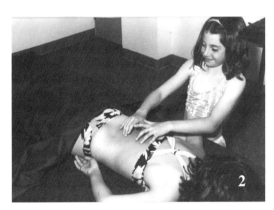

♥ (2) Using the fingertips lightly tickle the back all over.

♥ Finish with "tapping." You can "tap" for a long time here.

Get in touch.

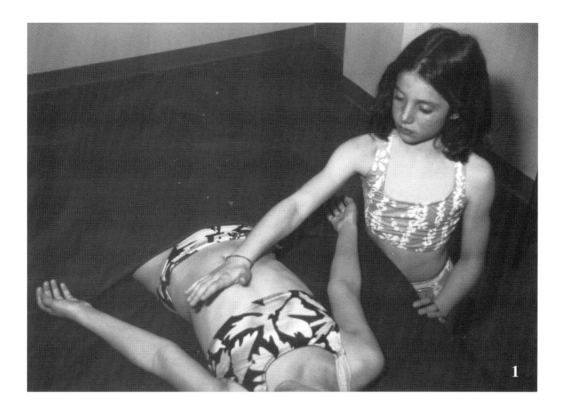

Belly
(Stomach and Abdomen Area)

Sometimes our deepest emotional tensions lodge in the stomach area. We might say things like, "I'm so scared, I think I'm gonna throw up," or "I'm so nervous I can't eat," or "That new boy spoke to me today and my stomach is in knots." Massage is something that can help ease that type of tension. Breath is another important tool. When you feel these types of tension in the stomach and abdomen, remember to breath deeply down into the belly. You might even try a few full belly breaths. (See page 16.)

♥ (1) Stand at the side of the table. Begin by using the heel of the hand to make large circles. Always go clockwise when massaging the belly. Start at the navel and move out. Do this 5-6 times. (Effleurage.)

♥ (2) Place hands along the side of the torso. Cup fingers around toward the back. Then begin to pull straight up. One hand comes right after the next. Start at the hip and go slowly up to the armpits, then back again. Do each side two times.

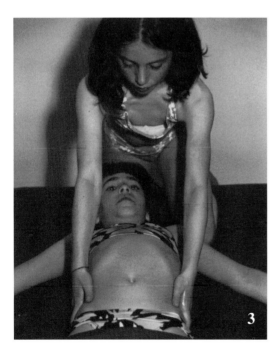

♥ (3) Last, reach under the waist on each side, into the back, as if you were going to pick up your friend at the waist. Now gently lift. Release. Lift again. Release.

♥ (4) Finish with tapping.

Head

Now you are ready for the head. We tend to carry a lot of tension in the head and neck from mental activity, worry, eyestrain and just plain thinking. It is also the part of the body from which we tend to be the most diconnected. Before you begin, ask your friend if she has any particularly tense or sore areas you might want to concentrate on. Begin with the face. Kneel or stand behind your friend's head. Remember to ask if oil on the face and in the hair is okay. Let your strokes flow from one to the next.

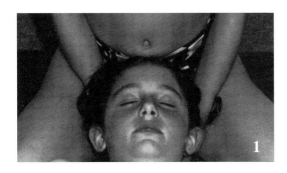

♥ (1) First cup your hands underneath your friend's head. Hold the head in your hands for a few moments. Connecting to your friend, and breathing fully, find your center. "Tune into" your friend—use intuition to try to get a sense of any energy blocks she may have in the body.

♥ (2) Without raising or turning the head, gently yet firmly pull the head away from the shoulders, stretching the spine. Release. Repeat.

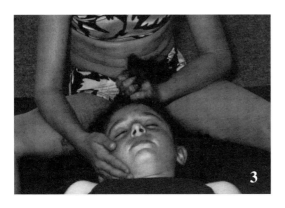

♥ (3) If the person you are massaging has fairly long hair, grasp the hair close to the roots and gently pull the hair. Release.

♥ (4) Massage the scalp. To finish, lightly tap the scalp and head all over with the fingertips.

♥ (5) Massage the forehead with your thumbs. Move in lines which cross the forehead from the center to the temples. Complete each stroke in a circular motion at the temple. Use firm, even pressure. Work this way in strips until you come to the eyebrows. Do the same across the eyebrows.

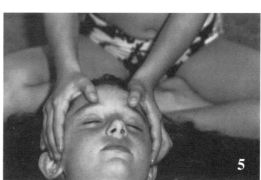

♥ (6) Next run your fingertips down the nose; then move fingertips, with firm, even pressure, out along the cheekbones to the ear. Do this several times.

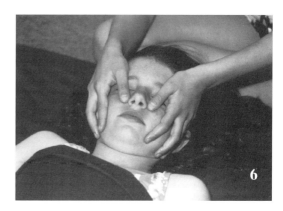

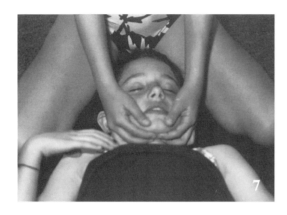

♥ (7) Move to the chin. Grasp the tip of the chin between the thumb and forefinger of each hand. Let your fingers follow along the jaw up to the temples using firm, even pressure. Move your fingers gently over the temples, making circular strokes.

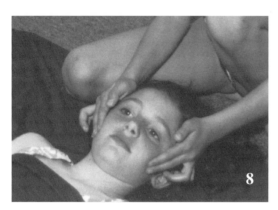

♥ (8) The jaw can hold lots of tension. The soft spot where the upper and lower jaw intersect is a hub for hundreds of energy points. Spend time massaging this area, varying the pressure and stroke.

Massage is an art.

Additional Strokes

♥ (1) Ear massage is wonderful. Run your fingertips behind the ears several times. Lightly pinch the outside of the ear from top to lobe. Gently pull the top of the ear up, the side of the ear out, and the bottom of the ear down.

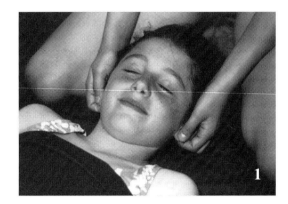

♥ (2) Ask your friend to listen to the quiet...Then slowly and gently close your friend's ear channels with the tip of your finger. Count to 15. Release slowly.

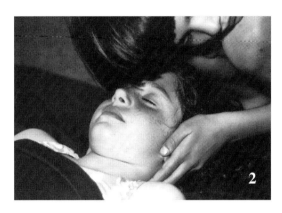

♥ (3) A great way to end: Rub hands briskly together until they feel hot. Cup hands over your friend's face. You may also experiment with cupping your hands and holding them over your friend's face without actually touching. This feels wonderful!

Neck

The neck has a big job: holding up the head. Because it often gets tired and sore, the neck needs *Tender Loving Care*.

♥ (1) To begin, cradle the head in both hands. Put your thumbs near the ears and let your index fingers meet at the base of the head. Your other three fingers of each hand rest on top of each other under the back of head and neck. Let the head rest there, keeping your hands spread this way. Hold for one minute or longer. This relaxes the whole body.

♥ (2) Cup your hands around the base of the head. Ask your friend to let all the weight of the head rest in your hands. Gently rock the head to and fro, about 15 times.

♥ (3) Lift the head with your fingers. Stretch the chin down toward the chest as far as possible.
Repeat 2 times.

♥ (4) Work the fingertips up and down the back of the neck. Go as far into the back as you can reach.

♥ (5) Now raise the head a little, lift, and turn the head slowly to the left until it rests on your left hand. Use your right hand to massage the neck, upper shoulder, and underneath the shoulder. Go up the back of the neck to the hairline and circle down the front to the shoulder. Use full, even strokes. This can be described as a figure-8 motion. Repeat this several times. (Effleurage.)

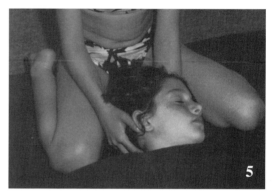

♥ (6) Use the fingertips to make small circles all around the neck, sides and back. (Petrissage.)

♥ (7) Feel for any tight spots. Use the thumb to firmly press into the area. Count to five, then release.

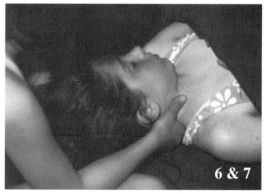

♥ (8) To finish this area, massage the scalp again or brush through the hair.

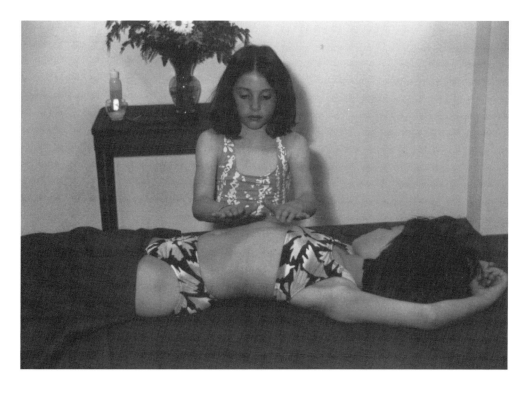

Ending a Massage

To end the entire massage, you may choose one or more of the following:

♥   "Tap" the whole body.

or

♥   Rub your hands together vigorously until they are quite warm.
Hold them over the face a few inches above
without actually touching the body.
You can do this over the entire body. This feels great!

and...

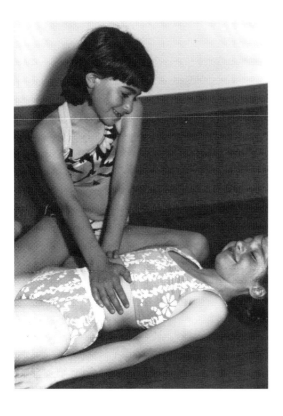

♥ If you have time, ask your friend if there is any last request. Call this "dessert."

♥ Remember: Always lift your hands away from your friend's body very gently. Remain silent for a few minutes. Sit silently or leave the room quietly while your friend relaxes. When your friend is up, then you can straighten up the space.

PART IV
Special Massages

Massage for Babies and Small Children

For an active small child, massage may sometimes be a welcome way to share quiet time together. Babies love massage. They probably won't hold perfectly still. That's okay. Experiment. Use a soothing voice. Try singing a lullaby. Light a candle and burn some incense in a safe place. You may find you and the baby in your life develop a special time each day for massage. Remember: very, very slow and very, very gentle massage for little ones.

Massage for Special Needs

Massage is a great way to communicate with friends or family who have special needs. For those who are blind or have speech or hearing impairments, the sense of touch may be more strongly relied on than it is for most of us. So massage may feel especially good. For those who may be retarded, or have physical handicaps or learning disorders, massage can help soothe damaged tissue and nerve endings. And massage is really nice for helping nurture and soothe in the face of the frustrations, sadness and emotional challenges that can be a part of disability. Remember—massage is about relationship. Don't be afraid to let your blind friend massage you, too. You may learn a thing or two.

Massage for Seniors

The next time you find yourself wondering what to give grandparents for their birthdays, try massage. Often as we grow older we lose "touch" with our loved ones. Many grandparents or great-aunts and uncles whom we dearly love live alone. They miss the hugs and playful games of tumbling they enjoyed when younger. They too need TLC. Offer a foot-rub while grandpa is reading the newspaper or grandma is knitting. Asking may feel a little awkward at first, and trying something for the first time often makes us a little embarrassed. Don't give up. After two or three tries you may find that massage time becomes a special time for laughter and stories—a time to share.

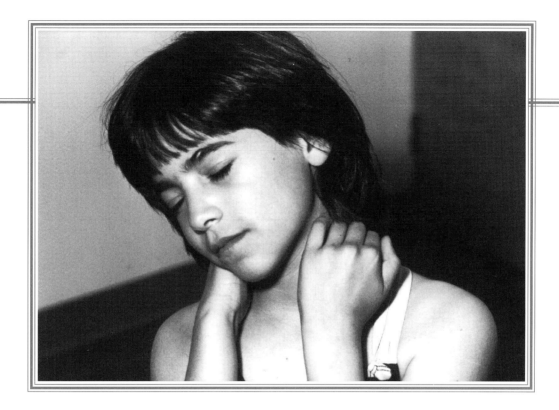

Self-Massage

Massage isn't only for partners. Many of the strokes can be adapted to use on yourself. Self-massage is a great way to manage stress that builds up from the pressure of tests, dance or theatre performances, try-outs for band or the team, and disagreements and misunderstandings with friends. One of the benefits of self-massage is that you can do it almost anywhere: in the classroom, waiting for the bus, even on the field. It's important to learn how to nurture yourself. Self-massage is a fun and simple way to do that. Here are some ideas to get you started. Experiment to find what feels best for you.

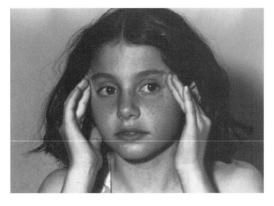

Headaches can often be eased by massaging the temples, jaws and eye sockets. Try vigorously brushing your hair with your head upside down, or massaging your scalp with your fingertips.

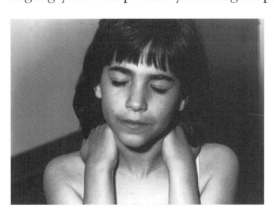

Sometimes you can actually get your own fingertips into tense spots in the neck and shoulders more accurately than someone else. Remember to be ever so kind to those tired, achy places. Your body will thank you for a gentle touch.

Self-massage can really help to loosen up your arms, wrists and fingers if you get writer's cramp, do gymnastics or play tennis or piano. When writing, for example, take a break between paragraphs and massage your arms, elbows and between the fingers. Remember to use your breath to help relax.

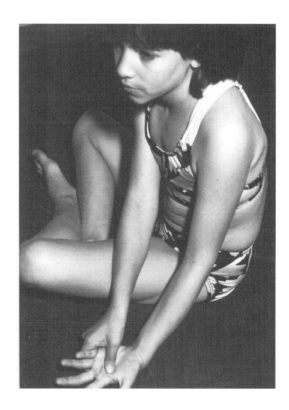

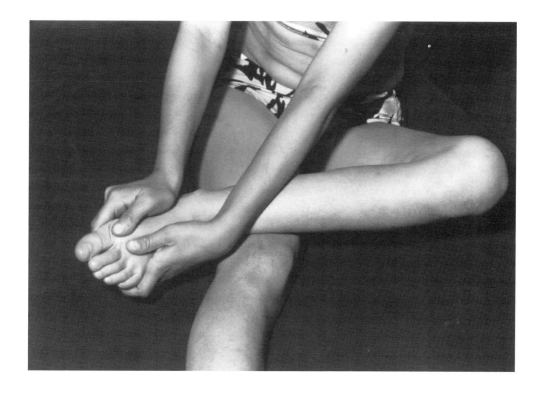

Experiment with foot rubs. Use the Foot Reflexology chart on page 57
to learn what spots on the feet correspond to other parts of your body.
For example: Where do you carry stress—in your head, neck or shoulders?
Then, gently massage the head, neck, or shoulder points on your feet.

You can give yourself a foot rub before slipping into your ballet or basketball
shoes. Sometimes just taking off your shoes, stretching the toes and rotating
the ankles can release a lot of tension, and set your feet to skipping rather
than dragging.

Foot Reflexology or Zone Therapy

To understand Reflexology, imagine the energy in your body as a huge network or web. See the strings of the web connected on one end to your organs, to parts of your nervous system, even to your joints. The other end of each string is connected to your feet. You know that if you pull on one end of a string something will happen at the other end. Reflexology is based on this principle. By massaging certain points in the feet, a corresponding organ or energy circuit can be affected in another part of the body.

Reflexology Chart

Use the chart below to explore foot massage for yourself or with a friend. Here's how: (1) Use the tips of your thumbs, or the knuckle of your index finger to massage the sole of the foot. Press firmly. Press everywhere. Go slowly. (2) When you find a spot that feels uncomfortably sore (if massaging a friend, he or she will probably say "ouch!" or pull away), then apply light pressure and massage in a circular motion for no more than 30 seconds at a time. Check the chart for the corresponding organ.

RIGHT FOOT*   **LEFT FOOT**

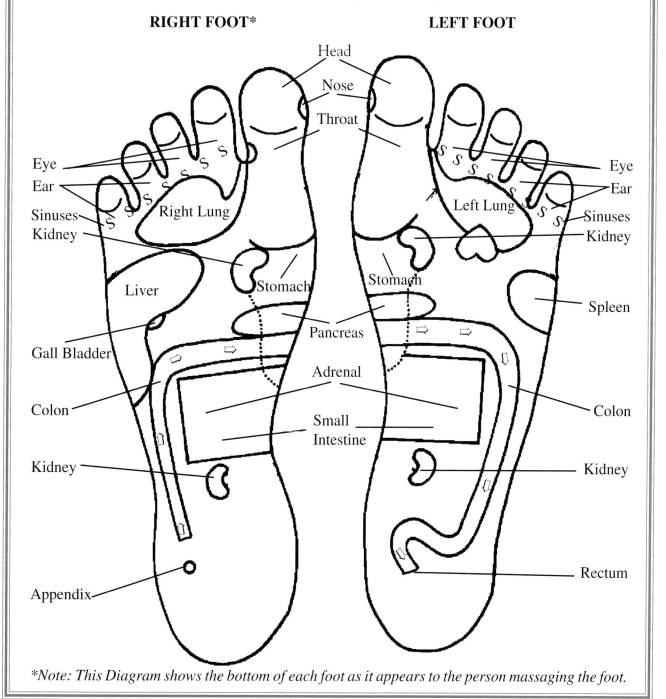

*Note: This Diagram shows the bottom of each foot as it appears to the person massaging the foot.

Conclusion

Learning the art of touch as a young person can only enhance your life as you grow. Self-awareness, sensitivity to others, and learning how to listen are key ingredients for happy, healthy relationships. Massage can help to develop these qualities. It is a way of offering nourishment which can feed the body and the soul. Other important aspects of nourishment are a healthy diet, exercise, a balance between work and play, and a commitment to expressing love and respect in our relationships. The sharing of massage can help to strengthen a foundation of caring relationship with our bodies, ourselves and each other. Listen to your body and learn to trust it. The body knows; if you listen you will learn untold truths.

Bibliography

If you would like to read more about massage, centering, and the art of touch, these are some books you could explore.

Baba Hari Das, *A Child's Garden of Yoga*, Santa Cruz, CA:
Sri Rama Publishing, 1980.

Rachel Carr, *Be a Frog, a Bird, or a Tree*, Garden City, NY:
Harper Colophon Books, 1973.

George Downing, *The Massage Book*, Berkeley, CA:
Random House-The Bookworks, 1972.

Gay Hendricks and Russel Wills, *The Centering Book*, Englewood Cliffs, NJ:
Prentice Hall, Inc., 1975.

Frederick LeBoyer, *Loving Hands*, New York, NY: Alfred A. Knopf, 1976.

Paul Reps, *Zen Flesh, Zen Bones*, Garden City, NY: Doubleday Anchor, 1961.

Deborah Rozman, *Meditating with Children*, Bouldercreek, CA:
University of the Trees Press, 1975.

Mary Stewart and Kathy Phillips, *Yoga For Children*, New York, NY:
Simon & Shuster, Inc., 1992.

About the Author

   Chia Martin is a mother, writer, and educator with a Master's degree in Special Education from Memphis State University. She has worked with children for over 20 years, including teaching young people with special needs and serving as a preschool teacher and director of a private school program. The idea for ***The Art of Touch*** came from her students. Chia is the author of ***We Like to Nurse*** (Hohm Press, 1994) and ***Rosie: The Shopping Cart Lady*** (Hohm Press, 1996). Her books are intended to promote caring, respectful, and harmonious relationships among children and adults, and to nourish the interrelated aspects of physical, emotional, mental, and spiritual growth.